Kid Pick!

Title: _____

Author: _____

Picked by: _____

_____

Why I love this book:

_____

_____

_____

Geology Rocks!

Minerals

EXPRESS EDITION

Rebecca Faulkner

Raintree

Chicago, Illinois

Produced for Raintree Publishers by Discovery
Books Ltd
Editorial: Kathryn Walker, Melanie Waldron, and
Rachel Howells
Design: Vctoria Bevan, Rob Norridge,
and AMR Design Ltd (www.amrdesign.com)
Illustrations: David Woodroffe
Picture Research: Melissa Allison and Mica Brancic
Production: Duncan Gilbert
Originated by Chroma Graphics Pte. Ltd
Printed and bound in China by
South China Printing Company

12 11 10 09 08
10 9 8 7 6 5 4 3 2 1

**Library of Congress Cataloging-in-Publication
Data**
Faulkner, Rebecca.
  Minerals / Rebecca Faulkner.
     p. cm. -- (Geology Rocks)
  Includes bibliographical references and index.
  ISBN-13: 978-1-4109-2774-3 (lib. bdg.)
  ISBN-10: 1-4109-2774-1 (lib. bdg.)
  ISBN-13: 978-1-4109-2782-8 (pbk.)
  ISBN-10: 1-4109-2782-2 (pbk.)
  1. Minerals--Juvenile literature. I. Title.
  QE365.2.F37 2008
  549--dc22

                          2006037172

This leveled text is a version of *Freestyle:
Geology Rocks: Minerals.*

Acknowledgments
The publishers would like to thank the following for
permission to reproduce photographs:

©Alamy p. **14** (Mark Baigent); ©Corbis p. **24** (Frank
Lane Picture Agency/Maurice Nimmo), p. **23** (Gary
Braasch), p. **28** (Jose Manuel Sanchis Calvete);
©GeoScience Features Picture Library p. **9**, pp. **12, 15
bottom, 30 right** (A. Fisher), p. **22** (D. Edwards),
pp. **11, 36** (G. Cook), pp. **5, 8, 10, 17, 33 top
left, 40, 41** (Prof. B. Booth); ©Getty Images pp. **5
bottom inset, 15 top** (National Geographic/Philip
Schermeister), p. **4** (Visuals Unlimited/Ken Lucas);
©Harcourt Education Ltd. pp. **6 all, 7 all, 34,
38 all, 39 all,** (Tudor Photography), p. **27 right**
(ISTOCK); ©Natural Science Photos pp. **21 bottom,
31, 37** (Martin Land); ©NHPA p. **44** (ANT Photo
Library); ©Rex Features p. **33 bottom right** (M. B.
Pictures), pp. **5 middle inset, 32** (Nils Jorgensen);
©Science Photo Library p. **43** (Alfred Pasieka),
pp. **19, 21 top, 25, 29 top** (Dirk Wiersma), p. **18**
(G. Brad Lewis), p. **13** (Martin Land), p. **42**
(Pascal Goetgheluck), p. **35** (Photo Library/Roberto
De Gugliemo), pp. **5 top right, 26** (TEK Image),
p. **30 left** (Wayne Scherr), p. **20** (Zephyr).

Cover photograph of salt pans in Italy reproduced
with permission of ©Getty Images (The Image Bank).

Every effort has been made to contact copyright
holders of any material reproduced in this book.
Any omissions will be rectified in subsequent
printings if notice is given to the publishers.

Disclaimer
All the Internet addresses (URLs) given in this book
were valid at the time of going to press. However,
due to the dynamic nature of the Internet, some
addresses may have changed, or sites may have
changed or ceased to exist since publication. While
the author and publishers regret any inconvenience
this may cause readers, no responsibility for any
such changes can be accepted by either the author
or the publishers.

CONTENTS

Some words are printed in bold, **like this**. You can find out what they mean by looking in the glossary. You can also look for them in the **On The Rocks!** section at the bottom of each page.

MARVELOUS MINERALS

What do a sparkling diamond, the salt you eat, and the tip of your pencil have in common? They are all minerals. Minerals are solid materials. They are found in nature.

Minerals come in all shapes and sizes. Some can be as large as footballs. Others may be too tiny to see. Minerals can be sparkly or dull. They can be very hard or soft and powdery.

Hard and soft
Diamond is the hardest mineral on Earth. Only another diamond can scratch it.

Graphite is the soft mineral used in pencils. It is so soft that it rubs off on your fingers.

⬇ **This is a mineral called smithsonite. It can be white, gray, yellow, green, pink, blue, or brown.**

graphite soft, dark mineral that is used in pencils

All rocks are made of minerals. There are more than 4,000 different types of minerals on Earth. Scientists are still discovering new ones.

We can see minerals all around us. They are in mountains. They are on beaches and in river beds. Some have amazing shapes. Others are very beautiful and valuable. Diamonds and rubies are worth a lot of money.

Find out later...

...how minerals are used in computers.

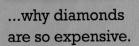

...why diamonds are so expensive.

⬇ **These rocks are called travertine. Travertine is made of the minerals aragonite and calcite. It forms from hot spring waters.**

...which mineral makes these icicle-shaped rocks.

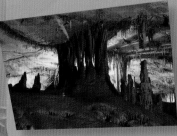

WHAT ARE MINERALS?

Rocks are made up of minerals. But what is a mineral made of?

A mineral is made of one or more **elements**. An element is a substance made up of tiny parts. These parts are called **atoms**. All the atoms in an element are the same.

Minerals usually form shapes called **crystals**. A crystal is a group of atoms. The atoms are

Eight elements

There are more than 110 elements. But most minerals are made up of these eight elements:
- oxygen
- silicon
- aluminum
- iron
- calcium
- sodium
- potassium
- magnesium.

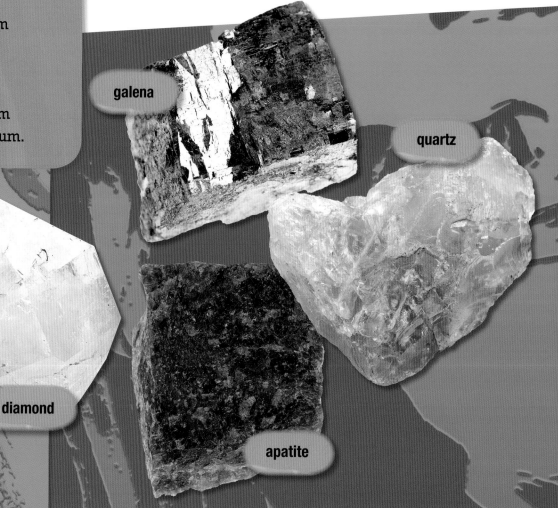

galena

quartz

diamond

apatite

crystal structure within a mineral

arranged in a repeating pattern. This pattern gives the crystal its shape. Crystals have smooth, flat sides. Some form cubes. A cube has six equal square sides.

Each mineral is always made of the same element or elements. It always has the same structure. For example, all diamonds are made from the element carbon. Their atoms will always be arranged in the same way.

⬇ Minerals come in a variety of shapes, sizes, and colors.

chrome diopside

topaz

hornblende

orthoclase feldspar

ROCKY MINERALS

There are more than 4,000 minerals on Earth. Only about 30 of them usually form rocks. These are called rock-forming minerals.

Rock-forming minerals can be divided into groups. The eight main groups are:

- native elements
- oxides
- sulfates
- carbonates

- silicates
- sulfides
- halides
- phosphates.

Hard mineral
Quartz (see page 6) is a very hard mineral. **Granite** is a rock that contains lots of quartz. This makes granite a hard rock.

⬇ **You can see the different minerals in this granite.**

element   natural substance made up of only one type of atom

Native elements

Most minerals are a mixture of **elements** (see page 6). But a few are made of just one element. These minerals are called **native elements**.

Most native elements are metals. Gold, silver, and copper are metals. They are native elements. They are usually found as **nuggets** (lumps) or flakes in rocks.

There are some native elements that are not metals. These include diamond, **graphite**, and sulfur (see the picture below).

Gold nugget
The largest nugget of gold ever found weighed 157 pounds (71 kilograms). It was found in 1869 in the country of Australia.

⇦ **Bright yellow sulfur is a native element.**

nugget   small lump of valuable material, such as gold

Silicates

Most rocks are made up of one group of minerals. These are known as silicates. Silicates all contain the **elements** silicon and oxygen. There are more than 1,000 different silicates.

Quartz, feldspar, and mica are very common silicates. Garnet and tourmaline are rare silicates. They are hard to find. These minerals come in many colors. They are used in jewelry.

Crusty minerals
Silicates make up more than 90 percent of Earth's **crust**. This is Earth's outer layer.

⇨ **This mineral is tourmaline. It forms long crystals (mineral parts). These long crystals can show two or more colors.**

Oxides

Oxides are another common group of minerals. They are made up of a metal combined with the element oxygen.

Hematite and magnetite are oxides. They both contain the metal iron. People used these minerals long ago to make tools and weapons.

Some oxide minerals are **gemstones**. Gemstones are minerals used in jewelry. Rubies and sapphires are gemstones.

Magnetic sand
You sometimes see black sand grains on beaches. These may be made of the oxide magnetite. If the black grains stick to a magnet, they are magnetite.

⇦ This dark mineral is magnetite. It is naturally **magnetic**. This means it can pull iron objects toward it.

Sulfides

Sulfide minerals are mixtures of the **element** sulfur (see page 9) and metals.

The minerals chalcopyrite and galena are both sulfides. They both contain useful metals. Chalcopyrite contains the metal copper. Galena contains the metal lead.

This is pyrite. It is a common sulfide mineral.

Sulfates

Sulfate minerals all contain the elements sulfur and oxygen. There are more than 200 sulfate minerals. They usually form when water **evaporates**. This is when water turns to gas. Gas is a substance like air. The water leaves behind parts of minerals.

All sulfates are soft and light in color. Gypsum is the most common sulfate. It has many forms.

Flower-shaped gypsum

Desert rose gypsum forms in deserts. Its petal-shaped crystals look like roses.

The gypsum in the picture below is called daisy gypsum. It has a daisylike shape.

Halides

Did you know that the salt you add to food is a mineral? It is called halite. Halite belongs to the group of minerals called halides. These are usually soft. They dissolve easily in water.

Halite forms as water **evaporates** (turns into gas). This happens in desert areas.

Carbonates and phosphates

The last two groups of minerals are carbonates and phosphates. Apatite is the most common phosphate mineral. Your teeth and bones are made of apatite.

Glowing mineral
Fluorite is a halide. It is a **fluorescent** mineral. This means that it can glow bright blue or green in the dark.

⇨ **The salt you add to your food is a mineral. It is called halite.**

stalactite   thin lump of rock shaped like an icicle. It forms as water drips from cave ceilings.

Calcite is a carbonate mineral. Water dripping into a cave may leave calcite behind. The calcite forms amazing icicle shapes (see the picture below). Those that hang from the ceiling are called **stalactites**. Those that grow up from the floor are called **stalagmites**.

⇨ **This is the mineral apatite. It is the most common phosphate mineral on Earth's surface.**

stalagmite short, stubby column of rock. It forms when water drips on to a cave floor and evaporates.

15

MINERAL CREATION

Most minerals form deep inside Earth. They form when hot liquid material cools. It then hardens into rock.

Earth is made up of different layers. The **crust** is like its skin. There are two types of crust. There are continental and oceanic crusts.

Continental crust is beneath land. It can be up to 45 miles (70 kilometers) thick. Oceanic crust is beneath oceans. It is up to 6 miles (10 kilometers) thick.

Rocky crust

Minerals make up the rocks of Earth's crust. We cannot always see these rocks. This is because they may be covered with water, soil, or buildings.

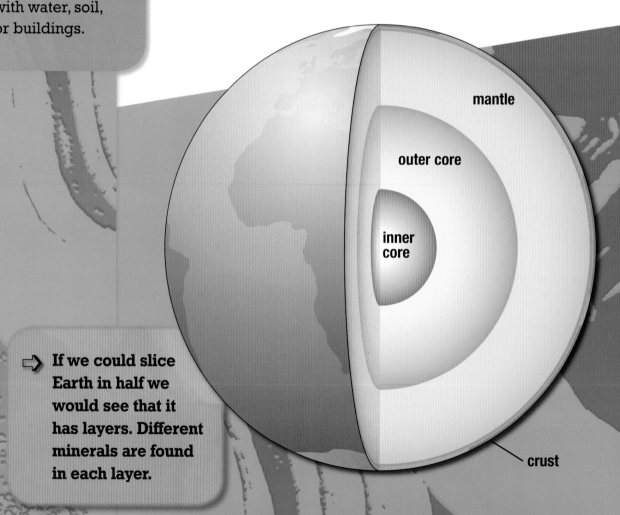

mantle

outer core

inner core

crust

⇨ **If we could slice Earth in half we would see that it has layers. Different minerals are found in each layer.**

Below the crust is the **mantle**. This layer is about 1,800 miles (2,900 kilometers) deep. The mantle is almost completely made up of silicate minerals (see page 10).

The **core** is at the center of Earth. It is even hotter here than in the mantle. There is a solid inner core and a liquid outer core. The inner core is made of hard metal. The outer core is melted metal.

Minerals in the mantle

Temperatures in the mantle are up to 5,500° Fahrenheit (3,000° Celsius). The rocks there are partly melted.

↑ The rocks of Earth's crust are made up of many different types of minerals.

How are minerals formed?

Earth's **crust** is made up of three types of rock:
- igneous rocks
- sedimentary rocks
- metamorphic rocks.

The minerals in these rocks form in different ways.

Igneous minerals

Minerals in igneous rocks are formed from **magma**. Magma is a hot liquid material. It forms in the layer of Earth called the **mantle** (see page 17).

⇨ Lava from volcanoes hardens when it cools. It forms igneous rocks.

Magma can take millions of years to travel up toward Earth's surface. As it does so, the magma cools and hardens to form minerals.

Minerals grow in shapes called **crystals**. Some magma cools slowly underground. This allows time for large crystals to form. The rock produced will have large minerals.

Some magma rises all the way to Earth's surface. It is called **lava**. Lava cools quickly. This allows little time for crystals to form. The rock produced will have small minerals.

⇩ **This granite has an unusual shape. It has been shaped by the sea waves over thousands of years.**

Sedimentary minerals

Some **sedimentary rocks** are formed from bits of other rocks. Wind and water break off tiny pieces of rock. They are carried to another place. Layers of these pieces build up over millions of years. They form sedimentary rock.

Some sedimentary rocks form by water **evaporating** (turning into gas). This happens near volcanoes and in deserts. The water leaves minerals behind. These minerals form sedimentary rock.

⬇ **This is Champagne Pool in the country of New Zealand. Its hot bubbling water contains lots of minerals. Some of them are gold and silver.**

Metamorphic minerals

Metamorphic rocks are rocks that have changed. They change because of heating or squashing.

When **magma** rises, it heats up the surrounding rocks. And movements in Earth's **crust** (top layer) squash and fold rocks over millions of years. This heating and squeezing changes the minerals in rocks. They become different minerals.

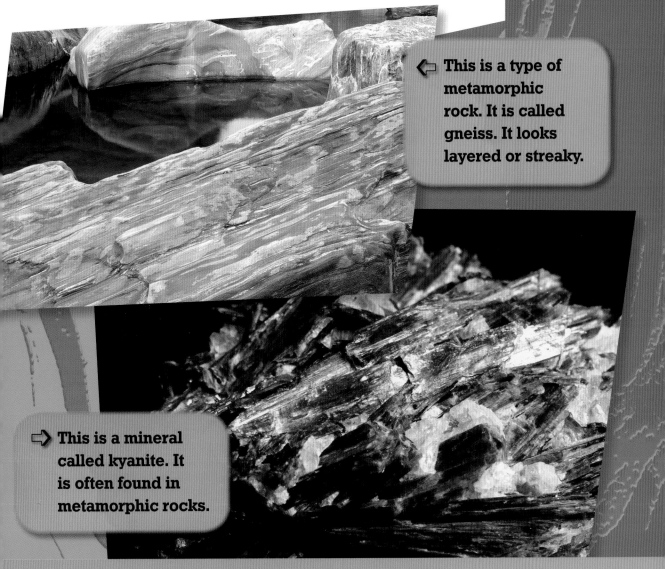

← This is a type of metamorphic rock. It is called gneiss. It looks layered or streaky.

⇨ This is a mineral called kyanite. It is often found in metamorphic rocks.

CRYSTALS IN CAVITIES

Crystals are solids formed by minerals. Some have amazing shapes. Some are very hard to find. They are rare crystals. The best places to find these crystals are in cracks in rocks. They are also found in **cavities** (spaces) in rocks.

Mineral veins

Rare minerals are often found in **mineral veins**. So are large crystals. Mineral veins are like sheets of minerals. They grow through rocks.

⬇ Carnelian is a rare mineral. Beautiful carnelian crystals are found in mineral veins.

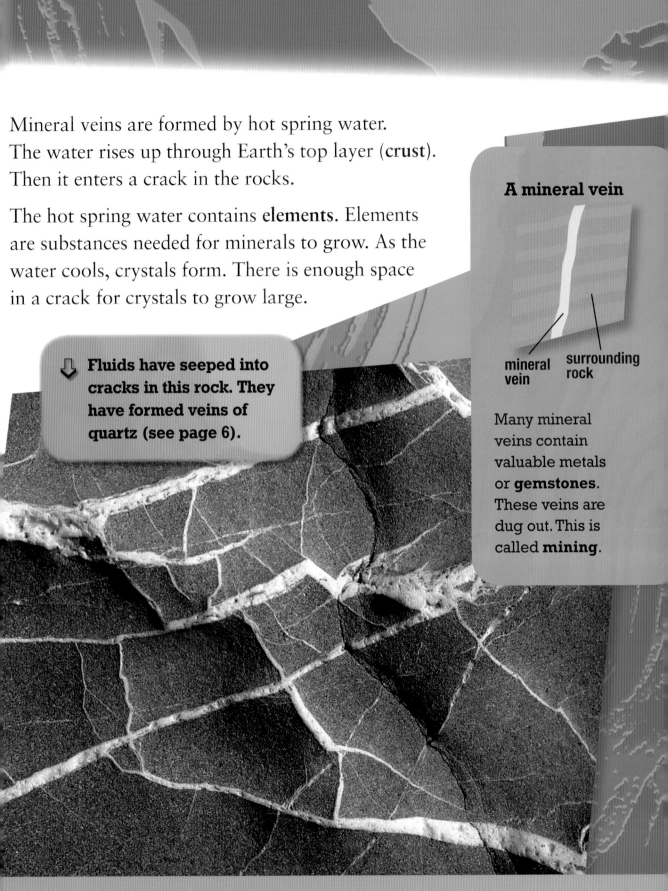

Mineral veins are formed by hot spring water. The water rises up through Earth's top layer (**crust**). Then it enters a crack in the rocks.

The hot spring water contains **elements**. Elements are substances needed for minerals to grow. As the water cools, crystals form. There is enough space in a crack for crystals to grow large.

⬇ **Fluids have seeped into cracks in this rock. They have formed veins of quartz (see page 6).**

A mineral vein

mineral vein   surrounding rock

Many mineral veins contain valuable metals or **gemstones**. These veins are dug out. This is called **mining**.

Geodes

A **geode** looks like a normal rock on the outside. But when a geode is split open, you see beautiful **crystals** inside.

A geode usually forms in volcanic areas. Hot **lava** comes out of a volcano. It often contains bubbles. Some bubbles get trapped as the lava hardens. They form spaces in the rock. These are called **cavities**.

Geode facts

The most common mineral found in geodes is quartz. Quartz comes in different shapes and colors.

⇨ Geodes like this are often found in the countries of Brazil, India, and Russia.

　geode hollow rock lined with crystals

Water picks up minerals as it passes through lava. This water may then become trapped in a cavity. Minerals from the water form crystals in this cavity. There is space there for the crystals to grow into beautiful forms.

Geodes are often round or shaped like an egg. The largest geodes are big enough to crawl into.

⇩ **The mineral agate is often found in nodules. It may contain fernlike patterns.**

Geodes and nodules

Geodes are rocks with a hollow space inside.

Round rocks that are completely filled with small crystals are called **nodules**.

nodule round rock completely filled with small crystals

How Important Are Minerals?

Minerals are very important in our daily lives. We use them to make many things. They make cars and computers. They even make toothpaste.

Uses of minerals

Some minerals contain metals that can be **extracted**, or taken out. These metals are used to make many things. They are used for spacecraft and tin cans.

Some minerals are very beautiful and hard to find. These are worth a lot of money. They include gold and silver. They also include **gemstones** such as diamonds and sapphires.

Did you know?
Fluoride is added to toothpaste to strengthen our teeth. Fluorides come from the mineral fluorite (see page 14).

⇨ **This is a silicon chip. It powers a computer. Part of the chip is made from the mineral quartz.**

Silica is found in the mineral quartz. It is used to make glass and silicon chips (see page 26). Silicon chips are used in many electronic items. They are used in coffeemakers and computers.

Talc is a soft mineral with many uses. Baby powder and paper contain talc.

(see page 26)

Colorful minerals
Some minerals have rich colors. These are ground into powder. The powder is used to make colored dyes for paints.

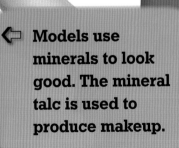

⇦ Models use minerals to look good. The mineral talc is used to produce makeup.

Metals from minerals

Some minerals are rich in useful metals. These minerals are called **metal ores**.

Chalcopyrite is the main metal ore for copper. Copper is a metal. It is used for water pipes and electrical wires.

Hematite and magnetite (see page 11) are important sources for the metal iron. Iron is used to make steel. Cars, airplanes, and ships are all made with steel.

Fool's gold

Pyrite and chalcopyrite are minerals that look like gold. Some people mistake them for gold. This is why they are sometimes known as "fool's gold."

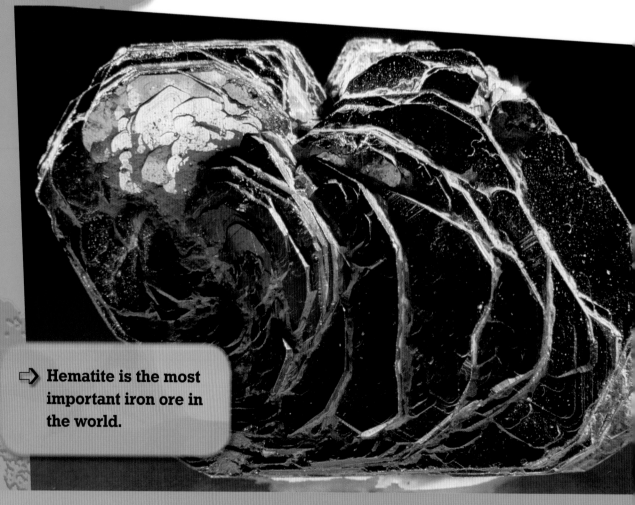

⇨ Hematite is the most important iron ore in the world.

metal ore mixture of minerals that contain useful metals

Metal ore is dug out of the ground. Then it has to be heated at very high temperatures. Heating separates the metal from the ore. This process is called **smelting**.

Some metals do not have to be separated from ores. This is because they are found in rocks as **native elements** (see page 9). A native element is a substance that occurs by itself. Gold and silver are found in this way.

⇐ Gold is found as **nuggets** in many types of rock.

Decorative minerals

Gemstone qualities

A gemstone has three qualities that make it different from other minerals. These are rarity, beauty, and hardness.

Minerals called **gemstones** are used in jewelry. The stones are cut and polished in special ways. This makes them sparkle.

The most valuable gemstones have special features. They are the hardest, most beautiful, and rarest gemstones. They are very hard to find. Diamonds and rubies are precious gemstones. So are emeralds and sapphires.

Other gemstones are known as semiprecious. These are not so expensive. They include garnets. Garnets can be

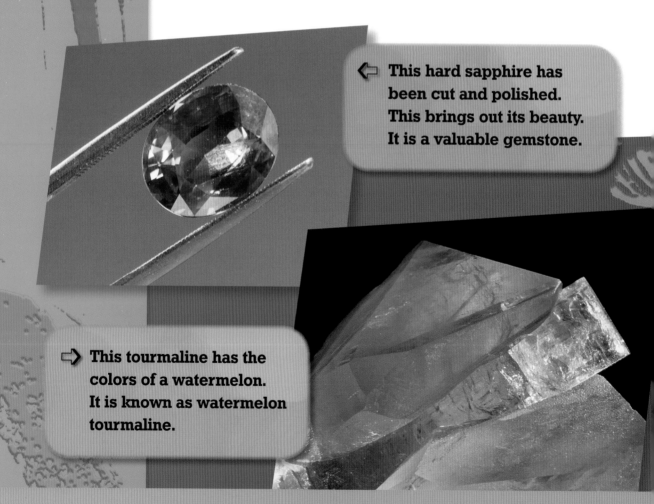

← This hard sapphire has been cut and polished. This brings out its beauty. It is a valuable gemstone.

⇨ This tourmaline has the colors of a watermelon. It is known as watermelon tourmaline.

a blood-red color. They also include tourmaline and topaz. These come in many colors.

Other minerals are also used for decoration. Jade and agates (see below) are used for ornaments. Agate has colored bands. Jade can be white, colorless, red, or green.

⇩ **This beautiful agate could be made into ornaments or jewelry.**

Gems from the deep

Diamonds are the most valuable **gemstones**. They are very rare. Diamond is the hardest known mineral. Light passes through it. This is why a diamond sparkles.

Diamonds form deep in Earth's **mantle** (see page 17). It takes millions of years for them to reach the surface. Diamonds are carried to Earth's surface in a rock called kimberlite.

Scientists group diamonds into the "Four Cs." The Cs stand for **carat**, clarity, cut, and color.

Diamond producers
Australia produces most of the world's diamonds. Diamonds are also found in South Africa, Brazil, and India.

⇩ **This is the world's largest uncut diamond. It weighs 616 carats. The diamonds you see in rings are usually less than 1 carat.**

- A *carat* is a measure of a diamond's weight. The more it weighs, the more it is worth.
- *Clarity* is how clear something is. *Clear* means free of marks. The clearer diamonds have more value.
- The *cut* is the special way of shaping a diamond to make it sparkle. A poor cut will make a diamond less valuable.
- Most diamonds have tiny amounts of *color*. A totally colorless diamond is very rare and expensive.

Diamond tools
Most diamonds are not suitable for jewelry. They are too small or an odd shape. But because diamonds are so hard, they are used in cutting tools and drills.

⇩ **A diamond's hardness makes it a useful cutting tool.**

⇨ **Diamonds are a favorite for jewelry because of their sparkle.**

carat measure of weight for precious stones, such as diamonds. It is also used as a measure of the purity of gold.

How Can We Identify Minerals?

Mineralogists
Scientists who study minerals are called **mineralogists**. They study the properties of minerals.

There are many different minerals. How is it possible to identify one? We need to look at its **properties**. A property is a feature that helps us recognize a mineral. Mineral properties include:

- color
- **streak** (its color when ground into a powder)
- shape
- hardness
- **density** (how heavy it is)
- **cleavage** (how it breaks)
- **luster** (how shiny it is).

⇨ You can be a mineralogist. Look closely at the rocks in your area. You may be able to see what minerals they contain.

property feature or quality of something that helps us to recognize what that thing is

Color

Some minerals are always the same color. For example, malachite is always green. Azurite is always blue.

Other minerals can vary in color. Pure quartz is colorless. But sometimes tiny amounts of other minerals enter the **crystal**. These are called **impurities**. When this happens, different colored quartz will be produced.

Colorful quartz

Impurities of iron in quartz can produce a purple color. This is called purple amethyst.

Pink rose quartz forms when there are impurities of the metal titanium.

⬅ **This is the mineral topaz. It can be found in many colors, including orange, pink, and green. It can even be colorless.**

impurity   invading substance that enters a crystal when it is forming

Streak

The **streak** of a mineral is the color of its powder. You can powder a mineral by scraping it against a streak plate. This is a type of hard white tile. Doing this will show you the streak color.

One mineral may come in different colors. But the streak color of that mineral is always the same. Quartz may be purple, white, black, or pink. Whatever its color, quartz always leaves a white streak.

Different streaks
- Pyrite has yellow crystals. Its streak is greenish black.
- Hematite is black. Its streak is brownish red.

⬆ **This spiky mineral is called millerite. Its crystals are a needlelike shape. This shape is known as acicular.**

Shape

Often we cannot see the **crystals** in a mineral. When we can see them, their shapes may help us identify the mineral.

For example, crystals of pyrite often form cubes. Cubes have six equal square sides. Crystals of quartz and **graphite** often form hexagons. These have six sides of equal length.

Sometimes the mineral shows no clear shape. Then we say it is massive.

Crystal shapes
Some common shapes of crystals are:

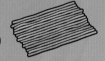 acicular (needlelike)

fibrous (threadlike)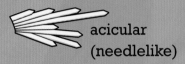

 mammilated (like rounded lumps)

botryoidal (like a bunch of grapes)

⇐ **This is the mineral malachite. Its crystals look like a bunch of grapes. This shape is known as botryoidal.**

Hardness

The hardness of a mineral is measured by how difficult it is to scratch. Diamond is the hardest mineral. Only another diamond can scratch it.

A **mineralogist** named Friedrich Mohs worked out a scale of hardness (see below). This helps people identify minerals.

Talc is the softest mineral. In Mohs' scale, it has a hardness of 1. Diamond has a hardness of 10. All other minerals fall somewhere between these two.

 This is Mohs' scale of hardness. Minerals below 3 are soft enough to be scratched by a fingernail.

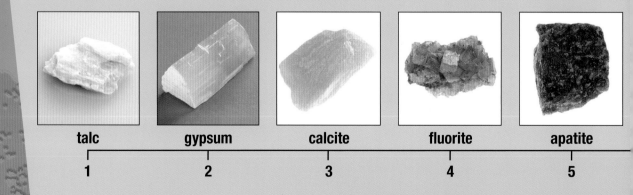

talc	gypsum	calcite	fluorite	apatite
1	2	3	4	5

Density

Density is how much something weighs compared with its size. All your mineral samples may be the same size. But some will be heavier than others. We say that the heavier ones have a greater density than the lighter ones.

Scientists can sometimes identify minerals by working out their densities. Gold is one of the most dense minerals in the world.

Mineral densities

Density	Mineral example
low density	sulfur, graphite
medium density	quartz, gypsum
high density	apatite, fluorite
very high density	galena, pyrite
extremely high density	silver, gold

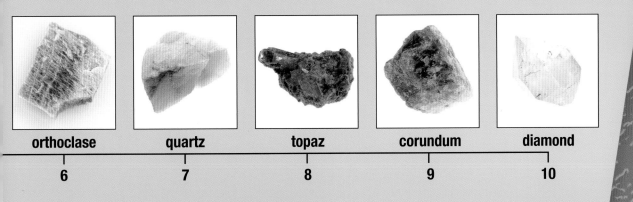

orthoclase	quartz	topaz	corundum	diamond
6	7	8	9	10

density   how heavy something is compared with its size

Cleavage

A mineral will always break in the same way. The way it breaks is called **cleavage**.

Some minerals break in only one direction. They usually come apart into flat sheets. Breaking in two directions produces long fragments. Breaking in three or more directions may produce cubes.

The directions of the breaks are called **cleavage planes**. Some minerals have no cleavage planes. They break in any direction and into different shapes. Quartz does this.

Cleavage planes

flat sheets

one cleavage plane

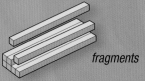

fragments

two cleavage planes

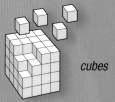

cubes

three cleavage planes

Minerals break into different shapes. The shape depends on how many cleavage planes there are.

⬇ Biotite mica breaks up into thin sheets. This is because it has one cleavage plane.

Luster

The **luster** of a mineral is a measure of its shininess. Some minerals shine like metal. We say they have a metallic luster. Diamond shines even more. We call this an adamantine luster.

Some minerals do not shine at all. This is called a dull luster.

⬇ **Quartz shines like a glass. This is called a vitreous luster.**

Types of luster

Luster	Appearance
adamantine	sparkly
greasy	shiny, oily
metallic	shiny, metal-like
pearly	shimmery like pearls
resinous	resinlike
silky	shimmery like silk
submetallic	uneven, shiny and opaque (not see-through)
vitreous	shiny, glasslike

Minerals under the Microscope

Mineralogists can find out what minerals a rock contains. To do this, they take thin slices of the rock. They look at them under a **microscope**. A microscope makes things look bigger.

The microscope makes it possible to see the different minerals in the rock. Mineralogists can then work out what the minerals are.

⇐ **This man is using a petrological microscope to look at minerals.**

42   **On The Rocks!**   microscope device used to see very small objects. It makes them appear bigger.

Mineralogists use a special type of microscope. It is called a petrological microscope. Petrological means to do with the study of rocks. This microscope can magnify minerals up to 2,000 times.

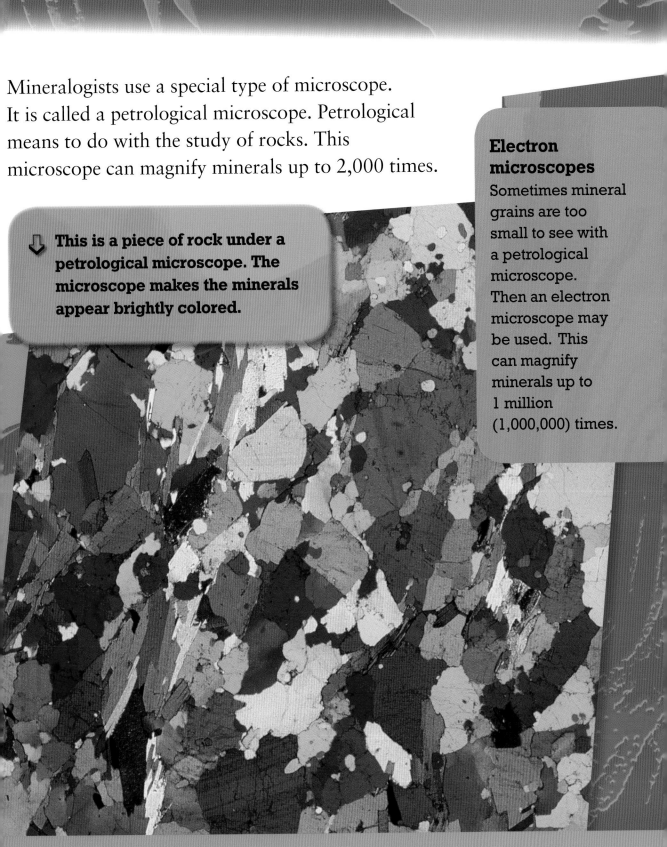

This is a piece of rock under a petrological microscope. The microscope makes the minerals appear brightly colored.

Electron microscopes
Sometimes mineral grains are too small to see with a petrological microscope. Then an electron microscope may be used. This can magnify minerals up to 1 million (1,000,000) times.

Summary

- Minerals are solid materials found in nature. They form rocks. The most common minerals on Earth are the silicate minerals.

- Most minerals form deep inside Earth. They form as hot liquid material cools and hardens.

- Minerals are made up of **elements**. An element is a substance made up of tiny parts. Different mixtures of elements form different minerals.

- The rocks of Earth's **crust** are made from about 30 minerals. But there are more than 4,000 minerals on Earth.

- Humans have **mined** minerals for thousands of years. Minerals have been used in all kinds of things, from paint and pottery to cars and computers.

⇨ Opal is a type of quartz that looks like colored glass. It is used in jewelry.

FIND OUT MORE

Books

Harding, Roger R., and Symes, R. F. *Crystal and Gem* (DK Eyewitness Books). New York: DK, 2007.

Morganelli, Adrianna. *Rocks, Minerals, and Resources: Minerals*. New York: Crabtree, 2004.

Squire, Ann O. *Rocks and Minerals* (True Books: Earth Science). New York: Children's Press, 2002.

Symes, R. F. *Rocks & Minerals* (DK Eyewitness Books). New York: DK, 2004.

Trueit, Trudi Strain. *Rocks, Gems, and Minerals*. New York: Franklin Watts, 2003.

Using the Internet

If you want to find out more about minerals, you can search the Internet. Try using keywords such as these:

- geodes
- diamonds
- mineral veins.

You can use different keywords. Try choosing some words from this book.

Try using a search directory such as www.yahooligans.com

Search tips

There are billions of pages on the Internet. It can be difficult to find what you are looking for. These search skills will help you find useful websites more quickly:

- Know exactly what you want to find out about.
- Use two to six keywords in a search. Put the most important words first.
- Only use names of people, places, or things.

GLOSSARY

atom tiny particle that elements and minerals are made from

carat measure of weight for precious stones, such as diamonds. It is also used as a measure of the purity of gold.

cavity a hollow or space inside something

cleavage how a mineral breaks up

cleavage plane line of weakness along which a mineral breaks

core center of Earth

crust thin surface layer of Earth

crystal structure within a mineral

density how heavy something is compared with its size

element natural substance made up of only one kind of atom

evaporate turn from water into gas

extract take out

fluorescent substance that glows in the dark

gemstone mineral that is cut and polished for use in jewelry

geode hollow rock lined with crystals

granite hard, igneous rock

graphite soft, dark mineral that is used in pencils

igneous rock rock formed from magma either underground or at Earth's surface

impurity invading substance that enters a crystal when it is forming

lava name for magma when it reaches the surface of Earth

luster how shiny a metal is

magma hot liquid rock from inside Earth

magnetic able to attract iron and other metal objects

mantle hot layer of Earth beneath the crust

metal ore mixture of minerals that contain useful metals

metamorphic rock rock formed when igneous or sedimentary rocks are changed by heat or pressure

microscope device used to see very small objects. It makes them appear bigger.

mine dig minerals out of the ground

mineral vein sheet of minerals that grows in cracks in rocks

mineralogist scientist who studies minerals

native element element that occurs naturally by itself

nodule round rock completely filled with small crystals

nugget small lump of valuable material, such as gold

property feature or quality of something that helps us to recognize what that thing is

sedimentary rock rock formed from the broken pieces of other rocks

smelt heat to a very high temperature

stalactite thin lump of rock shaped like an icicle. It forms as water drips from cave ceilings.

stalagmite short, stubby column of rock. It forms when water drips on to a cave floor and evaporates.

streak color of a mineral when it is powdered

INDEX